THE
FABULOUS
LOST &
FOUND

AND THE LITTLE FRENCH MOUSE

WRITTEN BY MARK PALLIS
ILLUSTRATED BY PETER BAYNTON

NEU WESTEND
— PRESS —

For Oscar and Felix - MP

For Hannah and Skye - PB

THE FABULOUS LOST & FOUND AND THE LITTLE FRENCH MOUSE
Copyright © 2020 Mark Pallis

ISBN 978-1-9160801-2-6
NeuWestendPress.com

THE FABULOUS LOST & FOUND

AND THE LITTLE FRENCH MOUSE

WRITTEN BY MARK PALLIS
ILLUSTRATED BY PETER BAYNTON

NEU WESTEND
— PRESS —

In the middle of the big city is a tiny yellow building. If anyone loses anything, this is where it ends up.

It is called the Lost and Found.

Mr and Mrs Frog keep everything
safe, hoping that someday every lost
watch and bag and phone and toy
and shoe and cheesegrater will find
its owner again.

But the shop is very small. And
there are so many lost things. It
is all quite a squeeze, but still, it's
fabulous.

One sunny day, a little mouse walked in.

"Welcome," said Mrs Frog. "What have you lost?"

"J'ai perdu mon chapeau," said the mouse.

Mr and Mrs Frog could not speak French. They had no idea what the little mouse was saying.

What shall we do? they wondered.

Maybe she's lost an umbrella. Everyone loses an umbrella at least twice, thought Mr Frog.

"Have you lost this?" asked Mr Frog.

"Un parapluie? Non," replied the mouse.

Then Mrs Frog remembered something that had been handed in a few months ago...

"Is this yours?" Mrs Frog asked, holding up a chunk of cheese.

"Du fromage? Non, ça pue!" said the mouse.

"Time to put that cheese in the bin dear," said Mr Frog.

"Maybe the word 'chapeau' means coat," said Mr Frog.

"Now where did I put that nice yellow one?"

"Got it!" said Mr Frog.

"Un manteau? Non. J'ai perdu
mon chapeau," said the mouse.

She was starting to feel a bit frustrated.

"We need to keep trying," said Mrs Frog.

C'est pas une écharpe.

Pas un pantalon.

Pas un pull.

Pas des lunettes de soleil.

Pas des chaussures.

"J'ai perdu mon chapeau," said the mouse.

Pas deux vélos.

Pas un ordinateur.

Pas trois livres.

Pas quatre bananes.

Pas cinq clefs.

It was no good. A fat wet tear rolled
down the mouse's cheek.

"How about a nice cup of tea?" asked Mrs Frog kindly.

"J'adore le thé. Merci," replied the mouse. They sat together, sipping their tea and all feeling a bit sad.

Suddenly, the mouse realised she could try pointing.

She pointed at her head.
"Chapeau!" she said.

"I've got it!" exclaimed Mrs Frog, leaping up.

"A wig of course!" said Mrs Frog.

"Non, c'est pas une perruque,"
said the mouse.

Pas rouge.

Pas blonde.

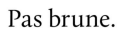

Pas brune.

Pas multicolore.

Pas verte.

"What about this?" asked Mr Frog, pulling back a curtain.

"Chapeau!" exclaimed the mouse.

"Ah, so 'chapeau' means hat. Wonderful!" Mr and Mrs Frog cheered.

Trop haut.

Trop petit.

Trop serré.

Trop gros.

"One hat left," said Mrs Frog, reaching all the way to the back of the cupboard.

"It couldn't be this old thing, could it?"

"Mon chapeau!

J'ai retrouvé mon chapeau!

Merci beaucoup," said the mouse.

And just like that, the mouse found her hat.

"Au revoir," she said, as she skipped away.
"Au revoir," replied Mr and Mrs Frog.

"I wonder who will come tomorrow?" said Mr Frog.
Mrs Frog put her arm around him.

"I don't know," she replied, giving him a squeeze,
"but whoever it is, we'll do our best to help."

LEARNiNG TO LOVE LANGUAGES

An additional language opens a child's mind, broadens their horizons and enriches their emotional life. Research has shown that the time between a child's birth and their sixth or seventh birthday is a "golden period" when they are most receptive to new languages. This is because they have an in-built ability to distinguish the sounds they hear and make sense of them. The Story-powered Language Learning Method taps into these natural abilities.

HOW THE STORY-POWERED LANGUAGE LEARNiNG METHOD WORKS

We create an emotionally engaging and funny story for children and adults to enjoy together, just like any other picture book. Studies show that social interaction, like enjoying a book together, is critical in language learning.

Through the story, we introduce a relatable character who speaks only in the new language. This helps build empathy and a positive attitude towards people who speak different languages. These are both important aspects in laying the foundations for lasting language acquisition in a child's life.

As the story progresses, the child naturally works with the characters to discover the meaning of a wide range of fun new words. Strategic use of humour ensures that this subconscious learning is rewarded with laughter; the child feels good and the first seeds of a lifelong love of languages are sown.

For more information and free downloads visit www.neuwestendpress.com

ALL THE BEAUTIFUL FRENCH WORDS AND PHRASES FROM OUR STORY

J'ai perdu mon chapeau	I've lost my hat
un parapluie	an umbrella
du fromage	some cheese
ça pue	it stinks
un manteau	a coat
une écharpe	a scarf
un pantalon	trousers
des lunettes du soleil	sunglasses
un pull	a jumper
des chaussures	shoes
un/une	one
deux	two
trois	three
quatre	four
cinq	five
un ordinateur	a computer
un livre	a book
une clé	a key
un vélo	a bicycle
J'adore le thé	I love tea
merci	thank you
une perruque	a wig
rouge	red
blond/blonde	blond
brun/brune	brown
vert/verte	green
multicolore	multicoloured

oui	yes
non	no
des chapeaux	hats
trop grand	too tall
trop gros	too big
trop petit	too small
trop serré	too tight
J'ai retrouvé mon chapeau	I've found my hat
merci beaucoup	thank you very much
au revoir	goodbye

> "I want people to be so busy laughing, they don't realise they're learning!"
> Mark Pallis

Crab and Whale is the bestselling story of how a little Crab helps a big Whale. It's carefully designed to help even the most energetic children find a moment of calm and focus. It also includes a special mindful breathing exercise and affirmation for children. Also available in French as 'Crabe et Baleine.'

Featured as one of Mindful.org's 'Seven Mindful Children's books'

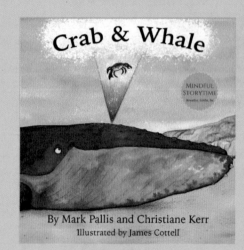

Do you call them hugs or cuddles?

In this funny, heartwarming story, you will laugh out loud as two loveable gibbons try to figure out if a hug is better than a cuddle and, in the process, learn how to get along.

A perfect story for anyone who loves a hug (or a cuddle!)

www.markpallis.com

You can learn more words and phrases with these hilarious, heartwarming stories from NEU WESTEND — PRESS —

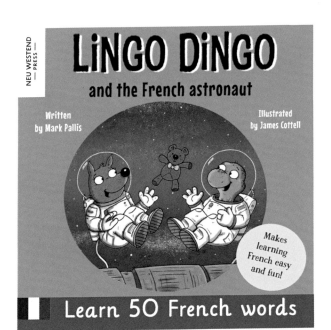

Made in the USA
Coppell, TX
26 June 2024

33915996R10024